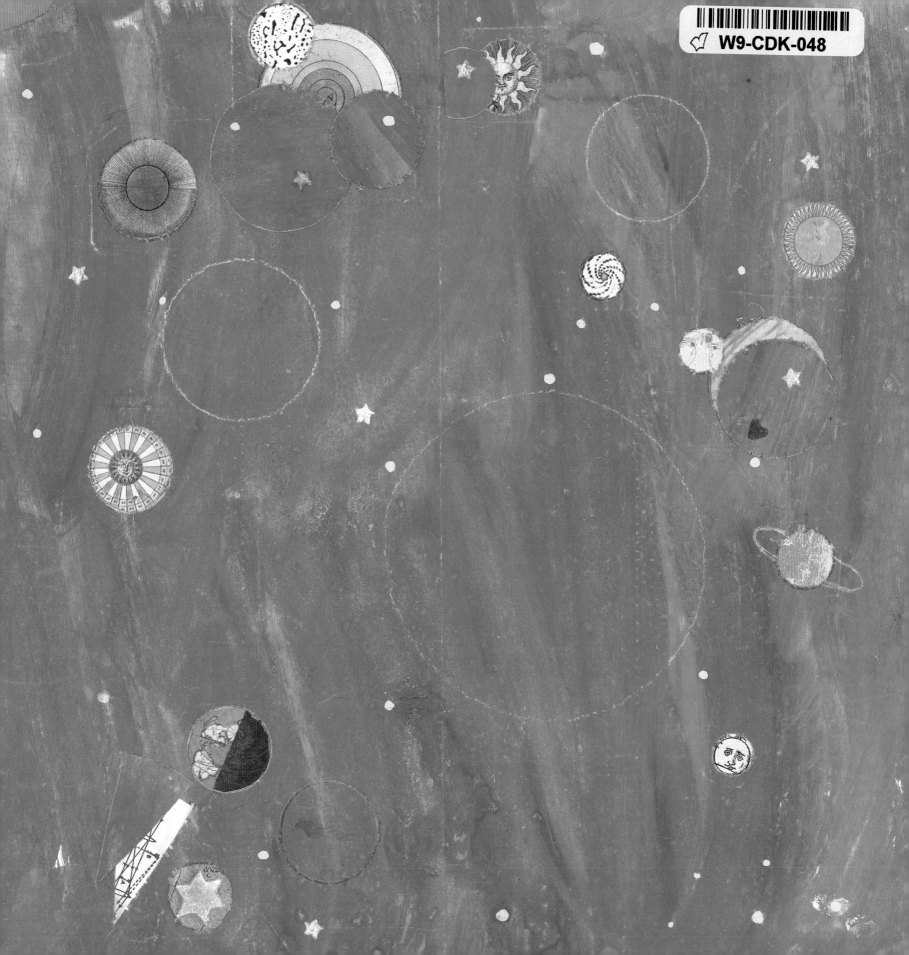

space poems and paintings by DOUGLAS FLORIAN

comets, stars, the moon, and mars

HARCOURT, INC.

ORLANDO AUSTIN NEW YORK SAN DIEGO TORONTO LONDON

MANUFACTURED IN CHINA

A LA MÉMOIRE DE ELI ABÉCASSIS — 1964-1986, CASABLANCA

EN FILS ATTENTIONNÉ, FRÈRE AFFECTUEUX, COUSIN CHÉRI DE TOUS
LIANT ET ATTACHANT, AMI SINCÈRE ET DÉVOUÉ
IL A TRAVERSÉ NOS VIES, SA DOUCE LUMIÈRE PARSEMÉE
ALTRUISTE, POÈTE ET MUSICIEN, FERVENT DE L'ÉQUITÉ
HABILE À L'ÉTUDE, AVIDE DE SAVOIR
OASIS DE BONTÉ, ÊTRE SANS AVOIR
UNE PARTITION D'AMOUR ET DE BONTÉ IL A JOUÉ

ELLE JOUE ENCORE POUR NOUS ET NOS PENSÉES POUR TOI TOUJOURS . . .

contents

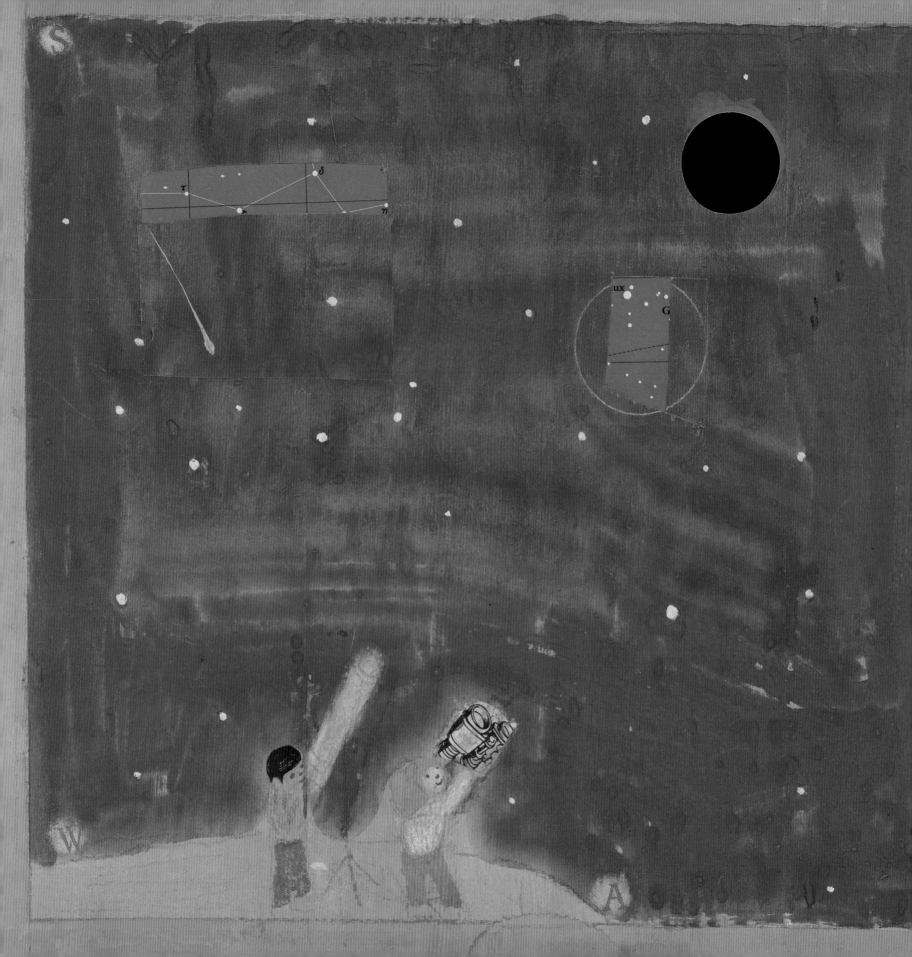

skywatch

On a clear night you might try
To gaze upon the starry sky.
A telescope or binoculars are
Great aids to observe a star.
To find your way it's good to sight
Upon a star that's very bright,
Like Sirius or Canopus,
Alpha Centauri or Arcturus.
You may see a planet or
A flash of light from a meteor.
Use a constellation chart
To help you tell the stars apart.
Start out when the day is done.
Most of all: Have lots of fun!

the universe

The universe is every place,
Including all the e m p t y space.
It's every star and galaxy,
All objects of astronomy,
Geography, zoology
(Each cat and dog and bumblebee),
All persons throughout history—
Including you,
Including me.

GALA... (margin letters)

a galaxy

A galaxy has stars galore: a million, billion, even more. Some galaxies are round, some flat. Some form spirals. Some seem far, and stars. Some have bars. All have stars, and stars. Some are egg shaped.

BARRED

BARRED SPIRAL

EGG SHAPED

the
solar system

Each planet orbits around the sun
(A somewhat circular path).
To calculate the time it takes
Requires lots of math.

Astronomers know the planets well,
Each mountain, ring, and moon.
But none has ever gone to one,
Nor will go to one soon.

SUN

SOARE

ZUN

LA

NAP

PÄIKE

the sun

Ninety-three million miles from Earth.
Nearly a million miles in girth.
4.6 billion years old.
Core eight times as dense as gold.
Here and there a dark sunspot.
And did you know . . . the sun is hot?

SOL, SOLE, ZON SONNE SHEMESH SAULE

SOL

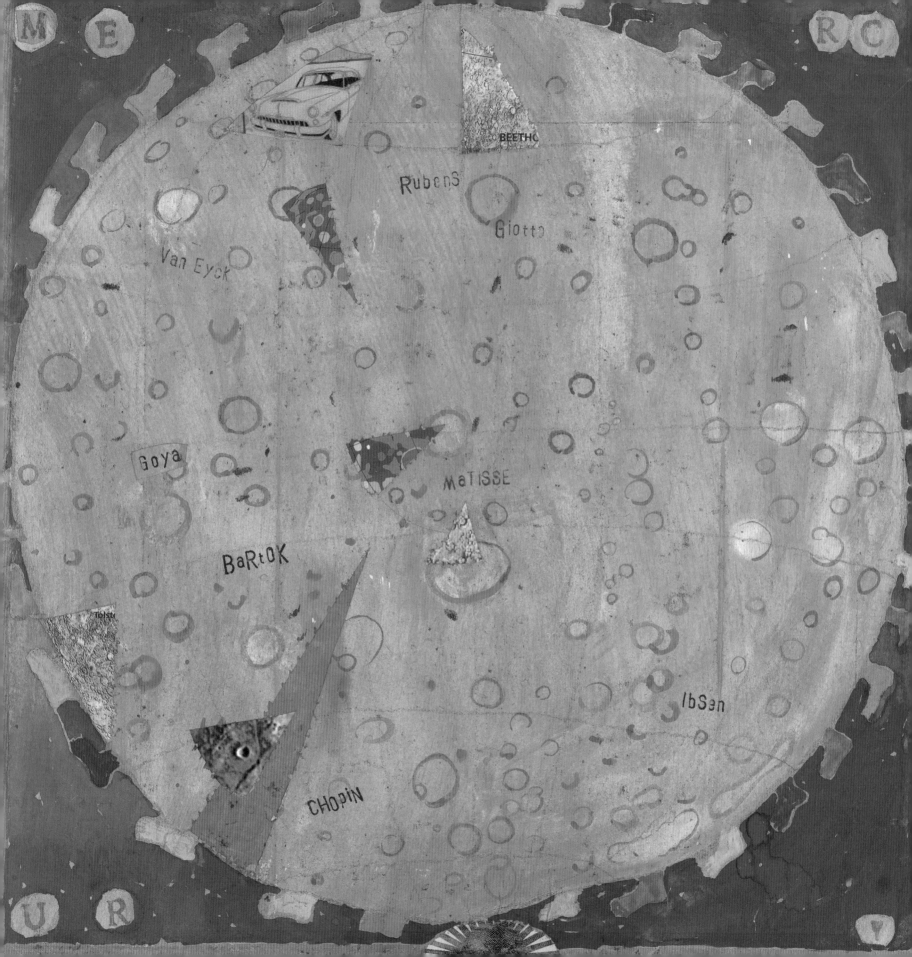

mercury

Speedy, nimble, quick, and fast,
Round the sun it rushes past.
Always racing, on the run . . .
You'd run, too, so near the sun.

venus

Scalding-hot surface,
Nine hundred degrees.
Nothing can live there,
No creatures,
No trees.
Poisonous clouds
Of acid above.
Why was it named for
the goddess of love?

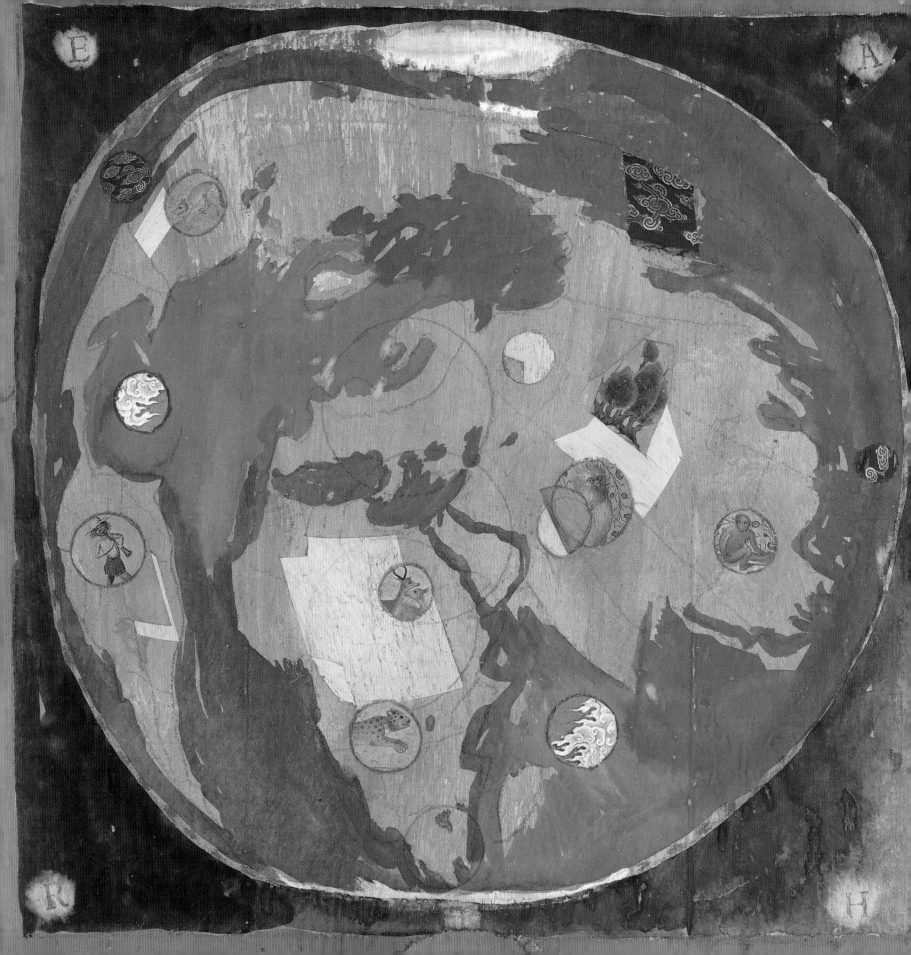

the eaRth

Two-thirds water.
One-third land.
Valleys deep.
Mountains grand.
Sky of blue.
Clouds of gray.
Life here, too—
Think I'll stay.

the moon

A **NEW** moon isn't really new,
It's merely somewhat dark to view.

A **CRESCENT** moon may seem to smile,
Gladly back after a while.

A **HALF** moon is half dark, half light.
At sunset look due south to sight.

A **FULL** moon is a sight to see,
Circular in geometry.

After full, the moon will wane
Night by night, then start again.

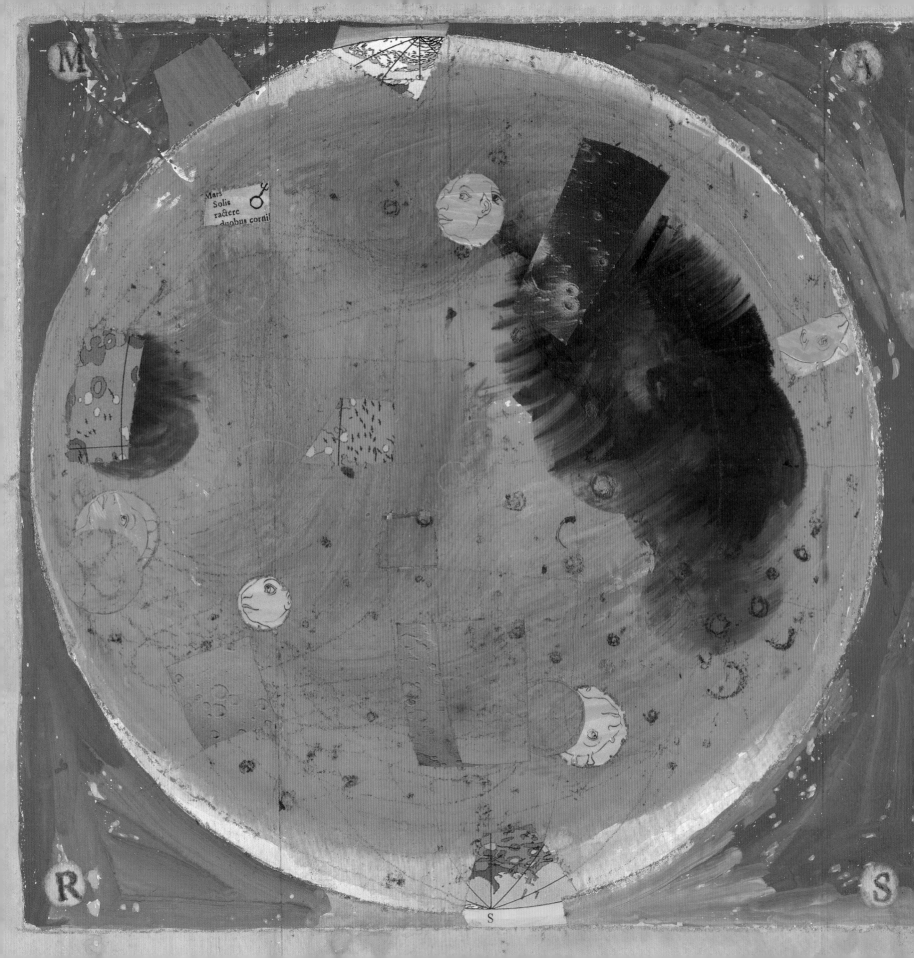

mars

Mars is red,
And Mars is rusty,
Sandy, rocky,
Very dusty.
Mars has ice caps.
Once had streams.
Mars has Martians . . .
In your dreams!

the minoʀ planets

Sometimes known as asteroids.
Sometimes called the planetoids.
They always help to fill the void
Tween Jupiter and Mars.

Named for sweethearts, daughters, sons.
Some are small as breakfast buns.
Others larger, weighing tons,
But none as grand as stars.

jupiteʀ

Jupiter's jumbo,
Gigantic,
Immense.
So wide
Side to side,
But gaseous, not dense.
With some sixteen moons
It's plainly prolific—
So super-dupiter
Jupiterrific!

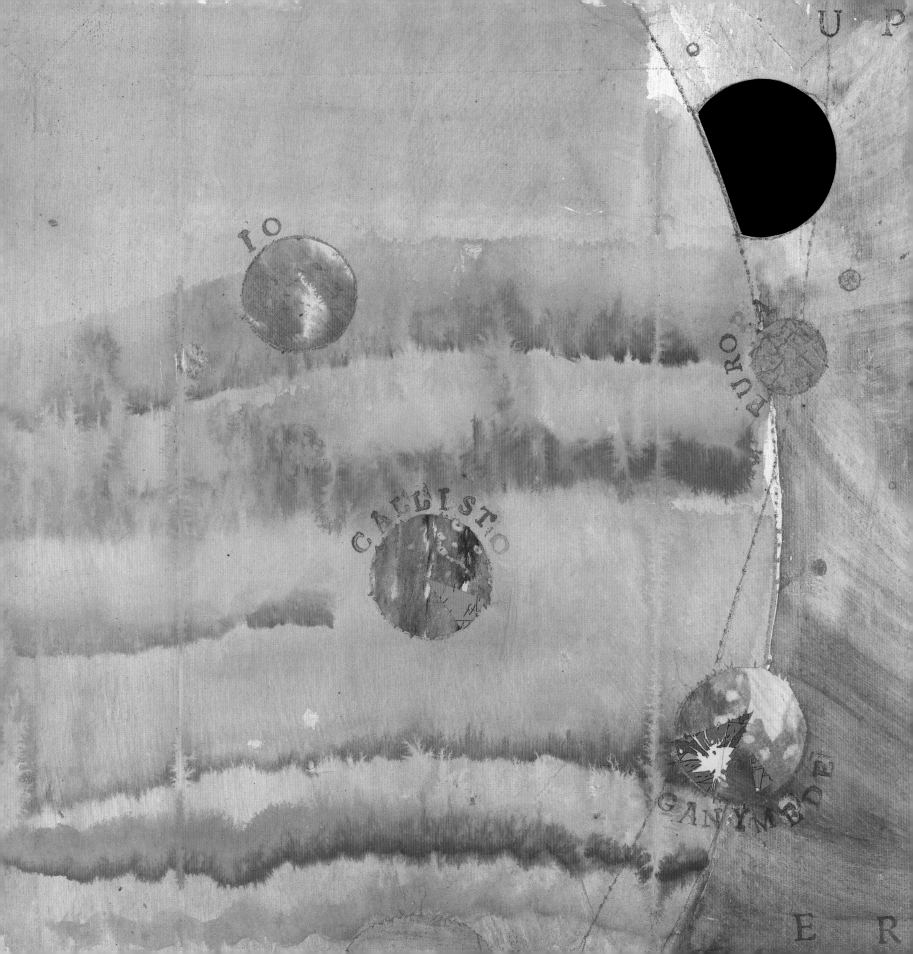

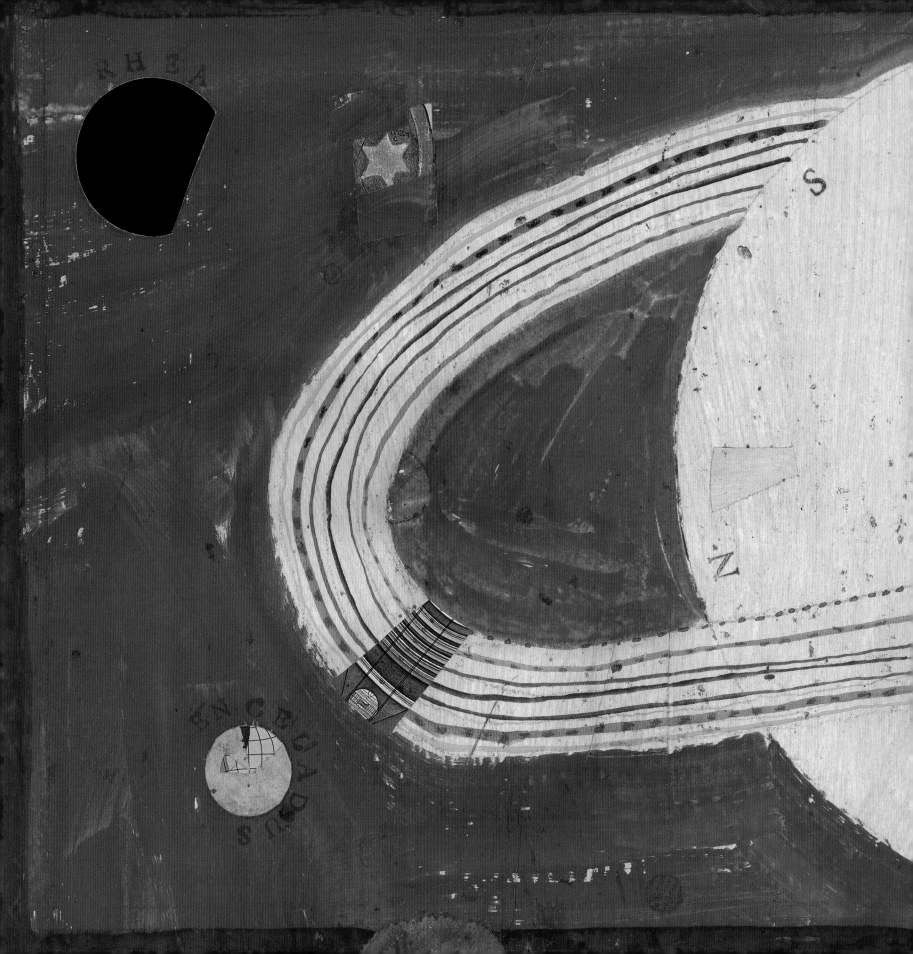

saturn

Saturn's rings turn round Saturn.
Its moons turn round it, too.
Saturn, by turns, turns round the sun.
Saturning through and through.

URaNUS

Counting up planets,
Uranus is seven.
Named for the Greek god,
Uranus of heaven.
Gaseous like Neptune,
But slightly more wide.
Heaven knows how
It got knocked on its side.

neptune

Named for the Roman god of deep sea,
So far out in space that it's quite hard to see.
Its rings were discovered by Voyager 2.
Neptune is frigid and freezing and

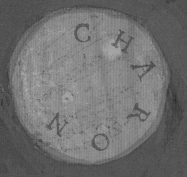

pⳑuto

Pluto was a planet.
But now it doesn't pass.
Pluto was a planet.
They say it's lacking mass.
Pluto was a planet.
Pluto was admired.
Pluto was a planet.
Till one day it got fired.

the comet

Ice, rock, dirt,
Metal and gas—
Around the sun
A comet may pass.
A dirty snowball
Of space debris.
The biggest snowball
That you'll ever see.

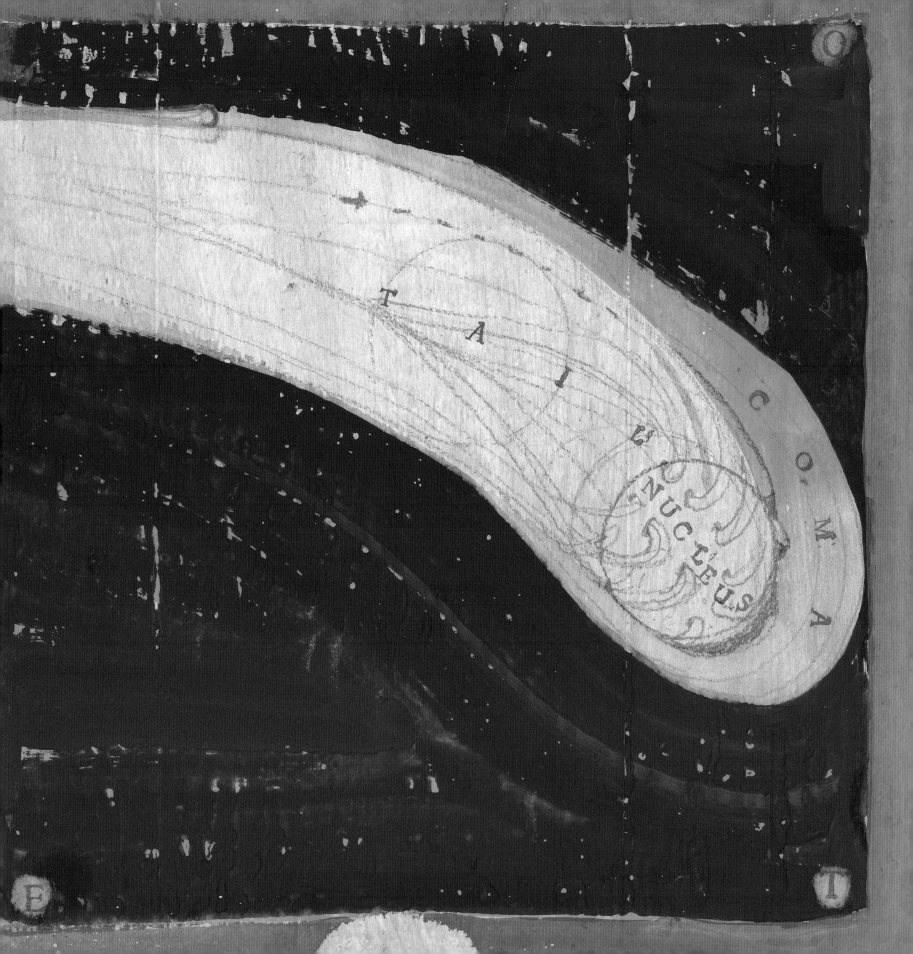

the constellations

Leo is a lion.
Lepus is a hare.
Cancer is a crab.
Ursa Major is a bear.

Lupus is a wolf.
Cetus is a whale.
Taurus is a bull,
From his horns down to his tail.

Pisces is two fish.
Musca is a fly.
And Cygnus is a swan
In this zoo up in the sky.

SUPER

NOVA

GAS

the BLACK hole

Nothing's black as
A black hole
(Not black ink or lumps of coal).
Some are small
And some quite wide.
Gravity pulls
All things inside
Like a giant
Cosmic broom.
(Wish I had one in my room.)

S

C

PLANET

PLANETOID

PLANETESIMAL

the great beyond

If you flew past Pluto
There's more that you'd see:
A planetoid, Sedna,
Found 2003,
And objects in orbit
Known as planetesimals
(Sometimes so small,
They're measured in decimals).
Great galaxies spin,
While bright comets race.
And I'd tell you more,
But I've run out of *space*.

P A

DECIMAL

DUST

E

A Galactic Glossary

SKYWATCH

Observing the night sky is a fascinating and awe-inspiring hobby. Binoculars will enable you to see the features of the Moon and all of the planets. A telescope has an even greater power of magnification that will allow you to study such distant objects as Jupiter's moons. Even if you don't have binoculars or a telescope, you can still enjoy skywatching. A sky map will help you identify the constellations as well as some of the planets.

the UNIVERSE

The universe is everything that exists in all of space and time—from the planets to the stars to the wide reaches of empty space. It contains billions of galaxies, each of which may contain billions of stars. Many scientists believe the universe was created ten to twenty billion years ago by a massive explosion called the *Big Bang*.

a Galaxy

A galaxy is a cluster of gas, dust, and millions, billions, or even trillions of stars that are held together by gravity. Some galaxies are so large it can take thousands of years for light to cross them. Earth is located within a galaxy called the *Milky Way*.

the SOLAR System

Our solar system, one of many in the universe, is made up of the Sun and all the objects that orbit it, including the planets and their moons, the minor planets (or asteroids), millions of meteoroids, and billions of comets.

the SUN

The Sun, the center of our solar system, is a sphere of spinning gas. Its energy is created by a nuclear reaction called *fusion*, which occurs when hydrogen atoms are changed into helium atoms. The Sun's surface is marked by dark patches called *sunspots* that are several thousand degrees cooler than the surrounding areas. The Sun is approximately 93 million miles from Earth and 29 million degrees Fahrenheit at its core.

MERCURY

The planet Mercury is named for the fleet-footed Roman messenger of the gods because it travels so quickly across the Earth's sky. Mercury is the closest planet to the Sun, and its craters are named after creative people, such as the composer Chopin, the artist van Gogh, and the writer Shakespeare.

VENUS

Often mistaken for a star, Venus is the brightest planet in the night sky because its cloud layer reflects most of the Sun's light. The planet's carbon dioxide–rich atmosphere acts as a thermal blanket, preventing surface heat from escaping into space. This *greenhouse effect* causes Venus's surface temperature to rise to almost 900 degrees Fahrenheit.

the earth

Earth, the third planet from the Sun, is the only place in the universe known to support life. It was thought to be the center of the universe until the Polish astronomer Copernicus discovered, in 1514, that Earth and the other planets orbit the Sun.

the moon

The Moon is airless and lifeless. Reflecting light from the Sun, it goes through phases as it orbits our planet, from *new moon*, when the illuminated side faces away from Earth, to *full moon*, when the illuminated side faces toward Earth. The Moon's surface is covered with craters that were formed billions of years ago when it was bombarded by meteoroids, asteroids, and comets.

MARS

Mars is named for the Roman god of war because its color reminded observers of blood. Its reddish hue comes from the iron-rich dust that covers most of its surface. While science-fiction writers have populated Mars with little green men, current research indicates that Mars does not support life. However, microscopic images from a Martian meteorite show structures that may be fossils of once-living organisms.

the minor planets

The minor planets, also called *asteroids* or *planetoids*, are pieces of rock orbiting the Sun. The largest is Ceres, which is approximately 580 miles across. The greatest concentration of minor planets is found between Mars and Jupiter in an area called the *asteroid belt*, where they likely number in the millions.

jupiter

The largest of the planets, Jupiter is named after the Roman king of the gods. It is a *gas giant*, a massive planet with a thick atmosphere made mostly of hydrogen and helium. Jupiter's Great Red Spot is a rotating gaseous storm that is larger than the Earth. It has been raging for more than 300 years and can be seen from Earth with a telescope.

saturn

Saturn, the second-largest planet, is best known for its rings, which are composed of billions of pieces of rock and ice. These pieces range in size from tiny specs to huge boulders. Although the rings appear very thin when viewed from the side, together they are more than 167,000 miles across.

uranus

The axis of Uranus, along with its moons and rings, is tilted 98 degrees. The planet was likely knocked on its side by a collision with another large celestial object. Uranus was the first planet discovered with a telescope. It was spotted by the British astronomer William Herschel in 1781.

neptune

Colored deep blue by the methane gas in its atmosphere, Neptune was named for the Roman god of the sea. It has eleven known moons, six of which were discovered, along with the planet's rings, by the *Voyager 2* space probe that flew past Neptune in 1989.

pluto

Most astronomers now say that Pluto is not a planet but rather a *dwarf planet*. It was reclassified in 2006 because of its small size, irregular shape, and unusual orbit. (It's tilted compared to the other planets and sometimes travels inside the orbit of Neptune.) Beyond Pluto lies a zone called the *Kuiper Belt*, which contains thousands of icy objects and perhaps dozens of other dwarf planets.

the comet

Sometimes called a dirty snowball, a comet's core or *nucleus* is made up of ice, rocks, and dust. Around the nucleus is the *coma*, a glowing cloud of gas and dust. When a comet comes close to the Sun, its frozen gases evaporate, forming a bright *tail*, which can be millions of miles long and visible from Earth. The famous Halley's Comet, named after the English astronomer Edmond Halley, passes by Earth approximately every 76 years and was last seen in 1986.

the constellations

Humans have been stargazing for thousands of years, connecting the stars into *constellations*, groups of stars in the shapes of heroes, animals, and objects. Astrologists believe that the mythological legends attached to the 88 constellations influence life on Earth.

the black hole

A large star may die in a huge explosion called a *supernova*. The remaining core might then collapse, forming a *black hole*, a dense area with such a strong gravitational pull that not even light can escape it. A black hole will suck in gas, dust, and even other stars.

the great beyond

Beyond the planets orbit many small objects including *planetoids* and tiny *planetesimals*. One such object was discovered by astronomers in November of 2003 and named Sedna. Beyond Sedna lies the *Oort cloud*, an enormous sphere of space containing billions of comets, some orbiting trillions of miles from the Sun. And beyond that lie other stars, other galaxies, and the vast, mysterious frontiers of space, which humans have yet to explore.

selected bibliography and further reading

✳ Chartrand, Mark R. *National Audubon Society Field Guide to the Night Sky.* New York: Knopf, 1991.

✳ Greeley, Ronald, and Batson, Raymond M. *The Compact NASA Atlas of the Solar System.* Cambridge: Cambridge University Press, 2001.

✳ Hawking, Stephen. *A Brief History of Time: From the Big Bang to Black Holes.* New York: Bantam, 1988.

✳ National Aeronautics and Space Administration. http://www.nasa.gov/home.

✳ Ridpath, Ian. *Stars and Planets.* London: Dorling Kindersley, 2002.

✳ Sobel, Dava. *The Planets.* New York: Viking, 2005.

www.HarcourtBooks.com

Library of Congress Cataloging-in-Publication Data
Florian, Douglas.
Comets, stars, the Moon, and Mars: space poems and paintings/
by Douglas Florian.
p. cm.
1. Outer space—Poetry. I. Title.
PS3556.L589C66 2007
811'.54—dc22   2006008274
ISBN 978-0-15-205372-7

H G F E

Manufactured in China

The illustrations in this book were done with gouache, collage,
and rubber stamps on primed brown paper bags.
The display type was set in Platelet.
The text type was set in Sabon.
Color separations by Bright Arts Ltd., Hong Kong
Manufactured by South China Printing Company, Ltd., China
Production supervision by Pascha Gerlinger
Designed by Douglas Florian and Scott Piehl